Dear Mare –

I think you'll enjoy this book
full of humor, love and a new
way of seeing life.

Nat, Sandy & I met the
woman author Ruth a couple
of years ago when we came
to Portland.

She is terrific & I hope —
And you can welcome the
book all you want to!

Love — Nelle

HOW TO BE AN ARTIST

STAY loose. learn to WATCH SNAils.
Plant impossible GARDENS. invite
someone DANGErous to teA. MAKE
little Signs that SAY Yes! and POST
them All over Your HOUSE. MAKE friends
with FreeDOM ¡ uncertainty. look FORWARD
TO DREAMS. CRY DURING MOVIES. SWING
AS HIGH AS YOU can On A SWINGSET,
BY MOONLIGHT. CULTIVATE MOODS. refuse
TO "Be responsible." DO iT FOR love.
TAKE loTS OF NAPS. Give MONEY AWAY.
DO iT NOW. THE MONEY will FOLLOW.
Believe in MAGIC. IAUGH A loT.
CelebRATe every GORGEOUS MOMENT.
TAKE MOONBATHS. HAVE WILD
iMAGININGS, TransFORMATIVE DREAMS,
AND perfecT CALM. DRAW On the WALLS.
reAD everyDAY. iMAGINE YOURSELF
MAGIC. GiGGle with CHILDREN. listen
TO OLD people. Open up. Dive in. Be free.
Bless YourseLF. Drive AWAY FEAR.
PLAY with everYTHING. entertain
Your inner CHILD. You Are innocent.
BUILD A FORT with BlanKeTS. GET WET.
HUG Trees.
write love letters.

♥ ©SARK 90

Inspiration Sandwich

or,

Stories to inspire our creative Freedom

BY SARK

BARNES & NOBLE BOOKS
NEW YORK

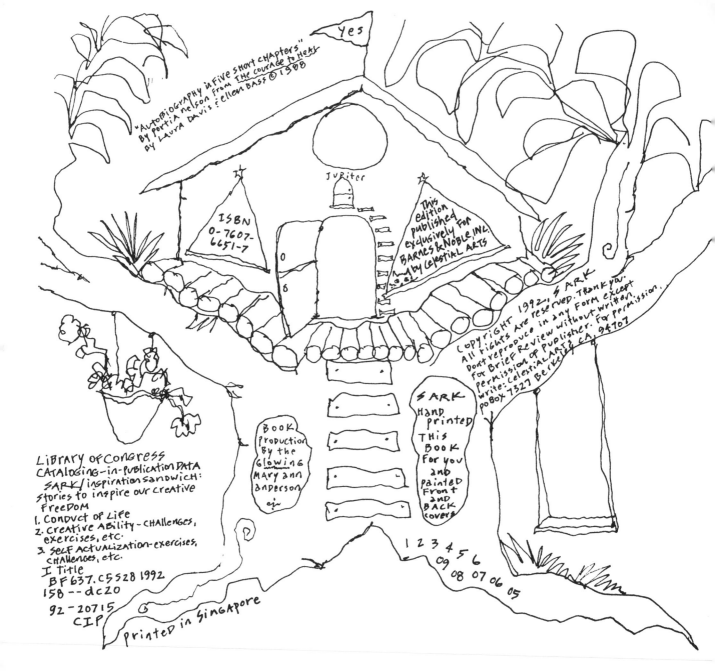

Yes

"Autobiography in five short chapters"
By Portia Nelson from The Courage to Heal
by Laura Davis & Ellen Bass © 1988

JUPITER

ISBN
0-7607-
6651-7

This edition published exclusively for BARNES & NOBLE INC. by Celestial Arts

BOOK
Production
By the
Glowing
Mary Ann
Anderson

SARK
Hand
printed
THIS
BOOK
For you
and
painted
Front
and
BACK
covers

LIBRARY OF CONGRESS
CATALOGING-in-PUBLICATION DATA
SARK / inspiration sandwich:
stories to inspire our creative
freedom
1. Conduct of Life
2. Creative Ability - Challenges,
   exercises, etc.
3. Self Actualization - exercises,
   challenges, etc.
I Title
BF637.C5 S28 1992
158 -- dc20

92-20715
CIP

1 2 3 4 5 6
09 08 07 06 05

PRINTED in SINGAPORE

THIS BOOK is FOOD For your SOUL, and A BUBBLE BATH For your spirit! It is A GUIDE to keeping your creativity ALive, and I wrote it for you.

In the SARK tradition, it WAS written while lying Down, in PAJAMAS, and in between nAps.

My First JOB WAS AT AGE 4 As the WAKe UP FAiry in KinDerGArten. I HAD A MAGic WanD, and touched eACH sleeping CHiLD. I still HAVe thAT MAGic WanD.

I Believe in WAKinG UP creative
spirits.

v

We are each inspired treasures, with creative gifts to share.

The world needs your gifts!

This book is meant to be nibbled and tasted in no particular order. If you can manage to be in pajamas while reading it, that would be wonder·full, and lying in bed with pajamas on is even better!

But, if you happen to be in the clothed, vertical world, at least take your shoes off.

Try this:
Pick a number between
one and forty-six

Then, turn to the following table of contents and see what chapter you've chosen.

There Are miracles All Around us

MirAcle:
an incandescent,
AMAZing event or
moment, Big or Small

The miracle is you

TABLE OF Contents

invite someone dangerous to tea

Cv.

While housesitting a mansion on Russian Hill in San Francisco, my neighbors told me I reminded them of a woman in the neighborhood.

"She's in her late eighties, and has art studios in her house and seems quite wild."

I called her, and introduced myself, and she said,

"Oh why yes, dear, why don't you come to tea on Thursday?"
That fabulous woman and I had tea every week for 5 years, and it was quite dangerous, indeed.

1

The Danger of entrancing
conversation, daring emotional
exchanges, and impossibly
delicious chocolate cake. We
formed a strong bond over tea,
over the years.

After her Death, I began hosting tea
parties at the St. Francis Hotel for other
Dangerous women.

We wear hats, and gloves, and tell
outrageous stories...

earl grey
with cream

Miriam's chair ♡

see
you
at the
Saint
Francis!

HUG Trees

Trees love Being HUGGED.
THe secret to HUGGinG trees is To
close your eyes so you won't FeeL
SHy. IF you HUG A
tree long enoUGH,
it will HUG you BACK.
Being HUGGeD BACK
Feels WARM and
BARKy. YOU MiGHT Grin.

Follow A Child

A child's world is made of spirit and miracles. We sometimes think that children should follow us, listen to us, become like us.

Follow A child closely for an hour. Not to teach or to discipline, but to learn, and to laugh.

My friend Edie and I were talking on the phone, when her two children Meredith and Claiborne, interrupted us with their shrieks and giggles. Edie said;

"Oh my God. They're stomping on Ritz crackers in their bare feet. Remember how good that felt? I can't watch.

I Don't want to stop them,
But I can't WATCH."
    SHe went into another room,
and we continued our conversation.
Her willingness to Allow Ritz
cracker stomping led me to write:
"How to really love A CHILD."

    My eight year old Friend, Stephanie
comes over to Draw on my walls and read
my newest writings.

    THis particular Day, I Felt angry
AT A Friend, and Decided to Ask
Stephanie's ADvice.

    "WHAT DO you DO when you're really
MAD AT A Friend?" I ASked.

She thought for a moment.

"Oh, that! Well. Usually you wait until one person forgets, and then that one calls up the other one and says 'Do you want to play?'"

Celebrate an old person
Cr.

We called my Grandfather "Boppa." When I was ten, He had a Playhouse built for me and installed in our Backyard. It had sliding glass windows, a tile floor, Dutch Doors and electricity! I was in ten year old Heaven.
I declared myself to be a writer and immediately "moved in" to my little House.
Then I decided I wanted a Horse and asked Boppa. He said;
"O.K. let's see about it."
He went and got a yellow legal pad and sat with me at the Dining room

tABle. We Began listing All the tAsks
anD expenses AssociAteD with owning
A Horse: BrusHing, FeeDing, exercising.
etc. Before long, the PAGe WAs completely
FUll, and I looKeD up anD sAiD;

"BoppA, I Don't think
I want A Horse After All."

He looKeD surpriseD, and
put the pAD AWAy.

There Are certain OLD people
wHo can HeLp you grow into yourseLF
Better. He WAs one.

CAre oF A Horse
1. FeeDing
2. BrusHing
3. exercising
4. SADDle Bridle
   Harness
5. SHoe repAir
6. STABles
7. HAy & ALFAlfA
8. VeT ATTention
9. CAre & ATTention expens
10. unexpecTeD expens

Swing as high as you can, on a swingset, by moonlight Cir.

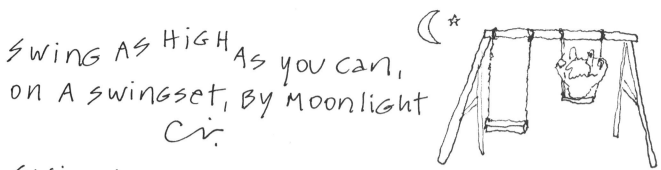

Swinging soothes nerves.
Swinging by moonlight is sacred.
Swing until your arms grow tired and your feet are ready to touch the earth again.

All your swinging memories will return. Remember the feeling of loving hands in the small of your back, pushing? Remember being afraid you would swing up and over the top? Remember letting go, and leaping off the swing, safely onto grass or sand?

Go ahead. Swing back into childhood...

WEAR PAJAMAS to A Drive in Movie

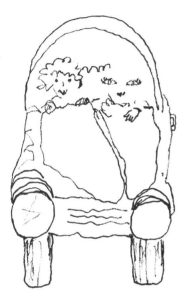

Just Before sunset, you were Bundled into your PAJAMAS and into the car, to A Drive in Movie. PerHAPS you laid on the car's WARM HOOD with an OLD Blanket or sleeping BAG, All snuggly in your PAJAMAS, on A WARM SUMMer night.

WEAr PAJAMAS More often! One time, I Boarded A plane in A Flannel nightGown and Hiking Boots. People Do stare, But only CHILDren Ask Questions. "Mommy, why is tHAT lADy in Her nightGown?"

In ChicAGo, my Friend and I had
to change planes, and I walked
through the Airport in that Flannel
nightgown.
A man passed us, jingling the change
in His pocket and smiling.
"Nice Pajamas!" He said.
My Friend responded,
"Hi, Bob!" I wondered How she
Knew Him, and asked Her.
"Didn't you recognize Him? That
Was Bob Hope

    anything can Happen in Pajamas.

DEVELOP an ASTOUNDING APPetite For BOOKS

BOOK recipes

I like to SAVOR and DiGEST A HEARTY selection of BOOKS: the smell of paper is an Appetizer. A DeeP Biography is GOOD with A Pinch of SHORT Stories, and A SAUce of romance novel Mixed Generously with an Assortment of essAys, travel stories and Memoirs. Simmer until SAUce thickens, and then ADD one strong SELF HELP BOOK. TAKE A NAP. Arise to stir up the Mixture and Begin AGain. entire AFFAir can Be BAKeD in 3-4 Hours AT A very HiGH TemperAture and SHOULD FeeD one Person until PleAsantly Stuffed. CAlories: 0. FAT: none. CARBoHYDRAtes: 0. P.S. Fiction and Poetry can Be ScAttered throuGHout and will vary FLAVor TremenDoUSLY.

learn to WATCH snAils

SnAils Are tiny prophets in our
GARDens. Moving slowly, cArrying
their own Homes, snAils Are kinD
to other snAils.
THere is A snAil in My GARDen I
cAll the "city snAil." Its sHell HAD
Been crusHeD or crAckeD, anD it
HAD Built A new sHell with PARt oF

A MAtcH Book tHAt SAiD:
Win $10,000! SnAiL WAtcHing
is Best By MoonliGHt, wHen
it is very lAte anD QvieT.

13

Wrap yourself in A thick Blanket, and sit down near some snails.

IF you're lucky, you might see them making love. one time, I laid on my stomach watching 2 snails make love for Hours. It looked so slippery and erotic, I felt shy! Later, I found out that snails Have both sets of sex organs!

IF snails ever Bother your plants, you can ask them to stop. Snails Are quite responsive to kind requests. or, if you have stubborn snails, make A compost pile just for them.

CATS Are angels with FUR.

Surrender, You Are now entering the tunnel of CAT love.

it's soft, it's WARM, it's CAT·A·Tonic.

Some little KNOWN CAT secrets: CATS Are POLKA DOTTED under their FUR. CATS love LEMONADE on A HOT DAY. CATS refuse to play SCRABBLE. CATS will PAY your rent if you let them. CATS HAVE not nine lives, but two; theirs, then yours. Some CATS MAKE PAY OFFS to FLEA GANGS. C.A.T. stands FOR Clever Anatomical Tricks. CATS KNOW HOW to cozy up. CATS sleep circular. CATS invented naps. Kiss your CAT. A FUR BALL is not A toy. ADOPT A CAT... it will TAKE over your Life (and you wont mind)

DEDICATED to: _____
(CAT name or names Here)

©SARK '91 (Dedicated to Jupiter the Yes CAT)

Kitty love   CAT NAPS

WILD CAT   CAT BUDDIES

DOGS Are Miracles with PAWS

A DOG'S nose in the PALM of your HAND
can cure ALMOST anything ✦ DOGS Are MADE
of love and Fur. ✦ Let your DOG TAKE you For
A WALK ✦ DOGS Are A sure thing ✦
some little known DOG secrets: DOGS
HAVE no secrets ✦ DOGS Are like vanilla
ice cream: reliably delicious ✦
DOGS Are wise Agents Directly From
Heaven ✦ if you HAD A tail, wouldn't
you WAG it? ✦ There Are no BAD DOGS
Be your DOG'S Best FrienD ✦ DOGS
Like Dancing, Drive-in movies and
Dreaming ✦ GOD MADE DOGS and
spelled His own name BACKWARDS!
DOGS MAKE GreaT THerapists
Kiss your DOG All the time ✦
some DOGS Are nap DOGS ✦ DOGS invented
unconDitional Love ✦ DOGS Are PARTY
Animals Apply DOG LoGic to Life:
eat well, Be loved, Get petted,
sleep A lot, DREAM OF A
LeASH-Free WorLD ✦

Live your DOG'S Life! ✦

miracle
(PAWS For A Miracle!)
P A W S

© SARK '91 DeDicated to Pussylina First dog love

DeDicated to: _____
DOG name or names Here

TAKE lots OF NAPS

I AM known As the "nAp queen." when I wAs in elementAry school, I would come Home For lunch, and For 42 minutes, chAnge into my pAJAMAS and tAke A miniAture nAp.

Naps Are necessAry to my creAtive life.

A good nAp can Be HArd to Find. sneAk AwAy, and set yourseLF up For the perfect nAp.

A smAll snAck, your FAvorite pillow, and A certain kind oF quiet.

cloud cover

17

Perhaps something to read, and if you can manage, a shaft of sunlight.

All at once, you sail away into a nap, where tangled nerves are untied, and where time stops.

Guilt and expectations are not welcome in napland. You can always find a reason not to take a nap. Find more reasons to let naps take you!

let the BOOK FALL SHUT

nAPS Forever

nAPland

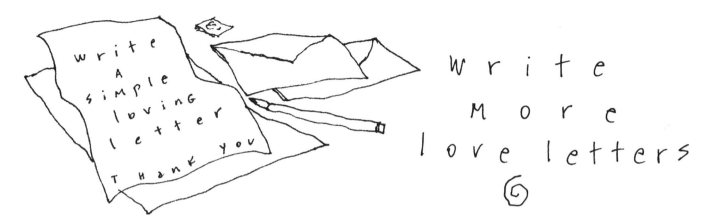

write
more
love letters

Letters Are cHances For the souL to speAK. A MooD cAptureD in the FiBers oF the PAper, A worLD in an envelope wHicH will not exist UntiL it is openeD.

Love letters MAKe love stAy VisiBle. You can ruB it, sMell it, toucH it, sHAre it, anD sleep with it UnDer your pillow.

Write A love letter on A BED SHeet
  with MAGic MARKers C⌒⌒⌒ sleep under it.
Write A love letter on the SIDeWALK
  with purple CHALK C⌒⌒⌒⌒ reAlly BiG.
Write A love letter in the SAND AND leAve
it to WASH AWAyC⌒⌒⌒.
Write A love letter to yourseLF, listing All
of your finest QUALities. RAve ABout you.
C⌒⌒⌒Then, MAiL it to your HouSe.
Write A love letter on A cotton SCARf with
InDiA inK. Give it to someone e⌒⌒⌒.
Design your own stAtioMery and use it C⌒⌒
MAKe A love letter BOX and Keep romAnce in it.

TAKE MOONBATHS

WALKING AT MIDNIGHT
is VERY GOOD FOR MoonBATHing.
I CARRY A WALKING STICK
AND BECOME invisible to
any trolls.
oNE noctuRNAL WALK, I
SAW A SMAll sign THAT SAID
"MAGiC CoTTAGE FoR A VERY
SPECIAL PERSON, SECLUDED
GARDEN with FERN trees."
I FOUND A COBBLED lane, and A MiniATURE
GATE with A STICK HOLDING THE GATE SHUT.
I PEERED INSIDE to see A SECRET GARDEN,
AND A tiny COTTAGE NEARLY HiDDEN BY PALM
FRoNDS. I knew it WAS MY HOME.

21

incidentally, I didn't have money, but I couldn't let that stop me from having a magic cottage!
I sold artwork, asked for favors and received help from family and friends.

Children often ask;

"Why is the magic cottage magic?"

I suppose it is because I believe in magic!

Allow yourself
to feel rich
without money

Many people who have
lots of money never feel
rich.
Feeling rich is born of simple things:
Good health, comfort, freedom and
laughter along with being well loved.
Money is important, but incidental.
Remember this affirmation: You
are welcome everywhere.
   I've been visiting Paradise Island
in the Bahamas for 20 years.

23

I USED to GO there without A DIME.

One time, I slept on A CHAISE lounge CHAir By the pool For 2 weeks! I GAVE My BAGGAGE to the ConcierGE anD CHanGeD into My evening clothes in the BAthroom.

WHen I MoveD to San Francisco From HAWAii, I HAD $35, So I FounD A BoArDinG House thAT CHArGeD $30 For the weeK.

Then, I FounD A FAMOUS anD elegant San Francisco Hotel loBBy to sit in anD DrAW.

I MADE A SMALL sign THAT reAD:
"ARtist AVAilAble for Dinner" anD SAT on
A wonDerful CHAir in the loBBy of the
Saint Francis HoteL with my sketchbook.
   Four sweet Guys from new york
SHOWED up and inviteD me to Dinner.

They HAD A corporAte
suite AT the HoteL thAT
wouLD Be empty the nexT
DAy, and AskeD iF I
wanted to occupy it!
(I DiD).

   Learn to step liGHTly
From one mirAcle to the nexT.
Feeling rich is AvAilAble to anyone,
AT any time. especiAlly to you!

25

EAT MANGOES NAKED

I ALWAYS LAUGH WHEN people WHO DON'T KNOW ME well, think I'M SO "FREE." Close FrienDS will tell you thAT I HAVE Many FeArs anD iDiosyn cRACies.

Just tAKe Mangoes. I DO not eAT theM NAKeD. It SOUNDS GOOD, But I Can't BeAr the thOUGHT OF enDUring thAT KinD of stickiness. one time, A FrienD in the BAHAMAS knew I WAS COMING anD FloAteD A lot oF Mangoes in My SwiMMing pOOL. THAT WAS the

only time I've ever eaten them
naked!
People frequently ask me about being
creatively alive and how to get
"unstuck." For myself, getting unstuck
is a daily, sometimes hourly, process.
I think it is about little things.
Altering your routine as much as
possible:

Buy purple flowers and put them
on a hat.

rake leaves and quit in the
middle.

Don't check your mail for 3 days.
Read the newspaper in the opposite order.
Break a dish you never liked.
Wear hideously colored socks.
If you're in a hurry, do things slowly.
These "little things" will lead you into a new mood.
A new mood will lead you into new creativity.
Then immediately take a nap and let it all soak in.

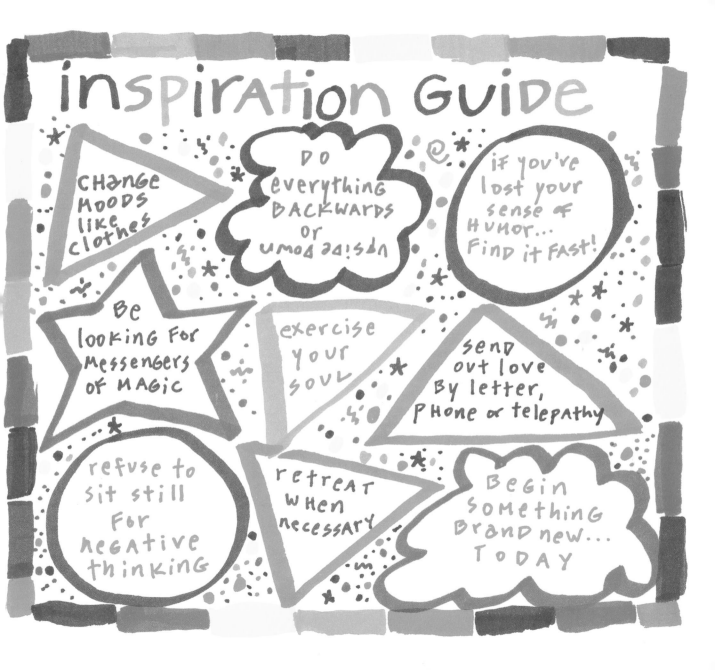

BUILD Forts with Blankets

Remember the safety of a good fort?
Bedspreads draped across chairs,
weighted down by giant books, with
a tunnel leading under the card table.
   Maybe there was a hole in one of
the bedspreads, put there so you
could peer out, unseen.

YOU MIGHT DRAG A STACK OF COMIC BOOKS
AND A ROW OF COOKIES into your FORT, AND
STAY THERE All DAY in the DUll GLOW OF
BEDSPREAD liGHT.
THE FORT WAS your
reFuGe, your secret
SPOT, The interior
untouched BY
ADULT HANDS or
eyes.
IT WAS A WORLD
you BuiLT FOR
yourself.
PerHAPS iF
your Best FrienD CAMe over, you
MiGHT MAKe enDless PLAYiNG CARD

Houses inside the fort, or eat so many Cheez Doodles that your face turned orange.

Now as an adult, I build forts with my cat Jupiter. We let the down comforters hang down all around the loft bed, and stay in there playing silly games.

Sometimes, we sing songs and snap rubber bands, and dream of a world filled with forts made of blankets...

Dry Your clothes in the sun

There is a rare smell that gets into clothes dried in the sun. It is a scent of waves and porches and summer grass. It is a fresh, luxurious, simple aroma that brings a smile and a hugging of the sheets.

There is a long wooden stairway that leads to my rooftop clothesline. The wind is always flag snapping off the bay, and I can look down

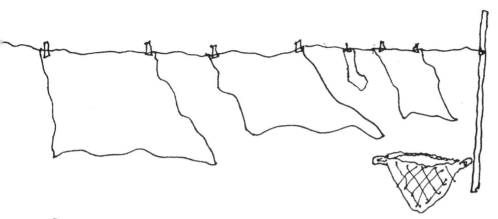

On the treetops. one time, I
stood up there For Awhile trying
to Figure out:
When exactly does that good smell
get into the clothes?
Like many good things, it is
mysterious and untraceable.

Drink sunsets

There is a tiny park in San Francisco that is perfect for watching the sun set. It's a bird's nest of a park up a long flight of steps made out of railroad ties. There are red tile rooftops and an assortment of brightly colored hummingbirds. I stand in honor of the sun retreating. I watch keenly as the light changes,

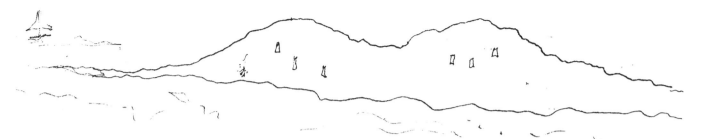

and windows glow golden across the
bay.
There is a certain purple sky in
san francisco that appears at
twilight. It is a color and shape
I never see anywhere else. I like
to observe the close of the day with
the sun's setting.

especially in a city, I think we
dearly miss nature if we don't
make a point to be there and absorb
her blessings.

How to take a miracle WALK

Bring A SMAll BAG
PACKED For extraterrestriAL
travel. WeAr A Brightly
colored HAT and pick A
Destination that Delights you.
   Along the way, communicate
with every aniMAL and CHiLD
you see. notice colors. DreAM
while MOVing. IF it's raining, this
counts AS A Double miracle WALK.
   WeAr an outlandish rain HAT
and stomp in every puddle you see.

Be open to the miracles. This means;
Follow your in·sight. Climb a tree,
peer over a fence, sit on a park
bench and wait ~ miracles are
some times shy.
Bring a notebook or sketch pad and
Position yourself in some extraordinary
spot. Let yourself be guided on paths
leading to miracles.
Let yourself "pleasure walk." No errands,
or time restraints. No plans!
anything could happen, and probably
will.
Here are the results of 3 of my "miracle
WALKS."

Greenwich steps 2:30 PM

I met her, as she crouched in a garden of baby tears, which is appropriate, since her mother was Grace Marchant, founder of the Marchant Gardens on the Filbert steps.

When I asked for her best gardening advice, she replied briskly, "Water, water and water some more! Rely on the earth to tell you what she wants, not some book!"

Valetta spoke of moving to Telegraph Hill "way back when" and paying $30 a month in rent.

"We didn't have much money for food, but we just had to have that cottage on the hill! Friends would bring sacks of potatoes when they came to visit us.

Now, of course, we own our cottage and these buildings around it.

I would tell anyone just starting out to,

"Hold fast to your dream!"

3:20 pm   PALACE   OF FiNE ARTS
Swans MATE for Life, WHICH Always MAKES Me HAPPY to Think ABout.
   THese swans encircle the PandorA ARt piece - an opening in
the wAter with stairs leading Down.
   I want to Fling myself into the pond and take those steps into
another world. A watery realm, A Fish PARADise, stAirwAy to
Neptvnian Heaven. THe swans in A singular Duet, their long
necks carving still pond waters. The light on the pond is A
certain luminous Green... Many spirits Have sat Here...

41

He calls Himself AGAPE, which means "love without ego" and He HAS Been Homeless By choice for fifteen years. He studies Lao Tzu, and plays the flute, and was once A professional photographer. He says "I got tired of "Human Doings" instead of Human Beings."
I asked if He ever gets uncomfortable Being outside, and He snorted and waved His arm at the passing crowd on Powell street. "Them! They're uncomfortable Being outside! Do you think they're examining any truths?"

Powell & Geary 5:20PM

42

extend surprising invitations

My friend Christina said to me, "Want to come over and eat poptarts and watch movies?"

I rapidly did an "Adult" calculation: Poptarts = A Headache, Movies = time spent doing "nothing."

Then, I let my "inside child" take over. Her house was set up as a movie cave. Futons, cushions and pillows covered the floor, and it was DARK, cool and quiet. Boxes of poptarts were stacked by the toaster. We bundled in and did nothing but eat poptarts and watch movies, and I loved every second! No Headache! We need to extend surprising invitations and accept them.

We told our friend Deidre to be
Available for a surprise on her 20th Birthday.
  Then, we picked a beach with an easy
3 mile trail leading to it, and hiked in
with a Table, white tablecloth, a vase of
spring flowers, candles, silver trays of
food, a birthday carrot cake, a bottle
of champagne, a white waiters jacket
(and a "waiter" to wear it) and a large
black umbrella. We set up this scene not
far from the edge of the ocean, and
not long before the sun's setting.

JoANN toLD Me sHe WANTED to GiVe Me A "MAGIC" tour oF BerKeley. I Got into Her CAr, anD FounD A white envelope With My name typeD on it. I openeD it to reAD:

"SARK's MAGIC tour oF Berkeley"

A wonDerous list FollowED oF encHanteD plAces to Visit.

AFter severAL Hours, I WAs lying on My BACK in A MAGnificent rose GArDen sAyinG,

"PleAse! I can't ABsorB any More MAGic!"

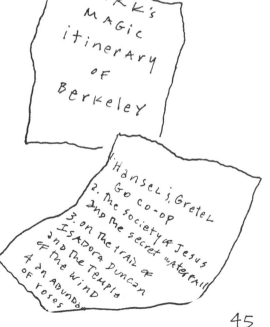

SARK's MAGic itinerAry oF BerKeley

1. HanseL ;, GreteL
2. Go co-op AND The society oF Jesus AND The secret wAterFAll
3. on The trAiL oF IsADorA DuncAn AND The TempLe oF The WinD
4. An ABunDo oF roses

FriendShips thrive on surprises. Make a Gingerbread Figure of Your Friend.
Send A letter to your friend with one Ballet ticket inside...
Meet Her there.
Give your Friend A Bag oF Fortune cookies — only you write All the Fortunes!

One of My Best Friends was named Miriam, and at the time she was 89 years old. I came to visit Her, and she opened Her Front Door to Greet Me Wearing A Gorgeous teal Blue Silk Suit.

I COMPLIMENTED Her anD SHe SAID
"Thank you" lAugHinG, anD Gently
stepped out of the Skirt anD took off
the JACKeT.
STAnDinG there in Her slip, SHe SAID,
"Here! I think it WOULD look GreAT
on you."

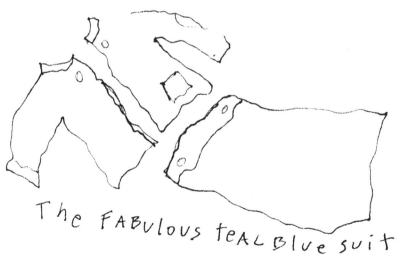

The FABulous teAL Blue suit

A MAZE YOURSELF

We ALL Do things thAT Are AMAZiNG.

I roDe A Bicycle 3,000 Miles and Felt AMAZeD the whole WAY.

My Brother andrew tALKeD me into CLiMBiNG HALF Dome in Yosemite the BACK WAY By trAiL ~ There is A CABle StAirWAY POUNDeD into the rocks and very steep. I Froze HALFWAY UP in A panic ATTACK and AMAZeD MyseLF By continuing to the top!

When it was time to write my First Book, I heard so many voices in my head that said, No! I amazed these voices by shouting Yes! and writing my book. Invite your fears in, then tell them to sit down and shut up!

When I first began getting massages, I felt very sensitive to pain, and asked for very light massages. Now, I am amazed to be having deep tissue bodywork and learning that conscious breathing can make pain go away.
I continue to amaze myself!

SHARe yourseLF on the teLepHone

SHe LiveD iN A PHone BootH

THis DrAWING is oF Me. I live aND lAVGH on the phone. Here Are soMe oF My "telephonic svggestions:" HAVe Fun on the pHone! IF you're HAVING Fun, the other person will Also, aND ABsolute MirAcles can tAKe place.

Secrets to HAVING Fun on The pHone: relax. BreAthe. lAVGH. let your personALity out to plAy. IF you're vsvAlly sHy, practice BeING BrAVe on the pHone. IF you GeT sCAreD, you can AlwAys JUST sAy GOODBye!

50

empathize with the other person: If
you're calling a car rental agency,
spend a few extra moments cheering
up and complimenting the rental agent.
   I imagine how you might feel being
at that job, and what you would like
to hear.

   Say something
slightly outrageous:
   We all want to
be delighted or
surprised.
   When I call for
an airline ticket,
I might ask if

Just remember:
everytime you
talk on the phone,
it forms a cartoon
bubble that floats
around for a long
time.

There's a special fare for people wearing raincoats or standing on their head at the airport. Then, the ticket agent and I can laugh together and become partners in finding the best ticket price. (I always fly at a great discount.)

Help people to become involved: If you can share something of yourself, people are much more inspired to help. Recently, I hired a tax consultant,

I JUST LOVE

You and me on the phone

and we agreed to work together by mail and phone. When I sent in my list of expenses and deductions, I enclosed a catalog of my work, with a photograph of me and a friendly note.

She loved the visual involvement, and now calls my answering machine with laughing messages, and our talks on the phone are easy and fun (yes, about taxes!)

Also, after doing my taxes, she sent me her bill, with a discount for my laughter, my answering machine messages, and my personality!

Have more fun with answering machines!

My phone is your phone... (except for long distance)

STAMP out Conformity! Leave no normal messages. We all know about leaving a message after the beep. Be experimental.

Remember to enjoy yourself while leaving someone a message. They'll hear the laughter in your voice and love to hear your words.

I like to think of my voicemail as "answering machine theatre:" A tiny electronic stage. I invent characters to "take the stage" and put on performances.

Currently, my message is just a recording of me laughing. It causes people to laugh in return, and we need it! Telephones are one electronic miracle after another.

answering machine theatre

Celebrate every Gorgeous Moment

I believe that I have developed a special sight for gorgeous moments. They occur around us all the time, in the most ordinary settings, but you must pay attention.

There is a bus driver I call "popsicles and broccoli" because he told me that he eats a lot of both to stay in shape. Mostly, he celebrates every person getting on the bus with an incandescent smile and words to help people laugh.

everyone HAS something Gorgeous to
offer if we take the time to listen.
  one time, while
riding A CABle CAr,
I HeArD A man say,
"I WAS the COOKie CAptain!"
I knew immediately WHAT
He WAS TALKING ABout, and
CAlleD out;
"I WAS the WAKe up FAiry!"
Soon, The whole CABle CAr Full of people
were CALLiNG out the "JOBS" They HAD
in KinDerGArten!
IF we reMeMBer THAT eACH OF US
HAS A SMAll CHilD insiDe, we can

Feel free to reach in and be truly friendly.

Miracles happen between people all the time, pressed into those tiny moments that might go unseen without "Miracle moment collectors"

Try walking around with an emotional net to capture Miracles in.

Then, share them with others.

We all need more Miracles!

Learn to be a radiant Human, and then shine on others.

I like to WALK, and Be GUIDED By MY
Feelings About wtere to GO.
On this DAY, I went into A BARBersHOP
BecAuse the BARBer WAS exuBerantly plAyInG
A clArinet.

He WAS Greek,
and Full oF JOY.
I sHAred some
Money worries
with HiM, and
He sAiD,

"ID rAther
spend one DAy
in totAL FreeDom,
than 50 yeArs
in PARTIAL cAptivity."
I leFt tHe BARBersHOP
very ricH.

DIMITRI'S
HAIR STYLING
&
BARBER
SHOP

Rich in my purpose and guided by my dream, floating on that "gorgeous moment."

I frequently ask God for "signs".
One evening, I was sitting in a small cafe, eating madeleine cookies for the first time.
I felt sad and confused about some issues and prayed for guidance.

I felt drawn suddenly to go into a bookstore and take a book from the shelf,
I opened the book to just this sentence:

"Whoever eats Madeleine's will be surely and certainly uplifted in all ways."

So here we are, in our rare and precious lives, surrounded by gorgeous moments begging to be noticed and celebrated.

Go! Celebrate!

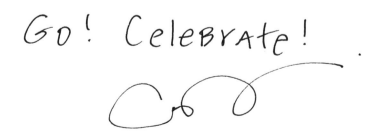

3PM
Golden Gate Park
Carousel

remember being
old enough to
ride alone AND
BACKWARDS?

61

MAKe FrienDs with FreeDom & uncertainty

One oF My FAVorite Heroes oF this type oF LivinG is naMeD RoBert. His LiFe is ConDenseD into A Few Boxes, anD the rest is Deep, ABunDant trAveL.

He Might return weArinG A cloAk woven in TunisiA, anD the next time you see HiM, He HAS Given it AwAy anD FounD another CoAt on A street corner.

His trAveL MoMents Are SHAreD in His WritinGs, PHotoGrAphs anD FiLMS. I BASK in His GLow oF FreeDoM anD uncertainty.

He is Constantly recreAtinG His LiFe, anD I Get nourisHMent FroM wAtcHinG.

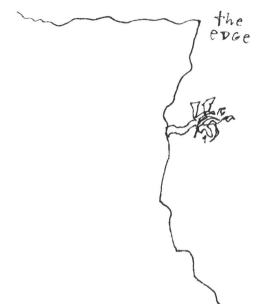
the edge

I believe that during my years of living "on the edge," I did learn to make friends with freedom and uncertainty, and that now I can reclaim that friendship whenever I begin a new book, or create something that has never been, before.

My very dear and delightfull friend Larry was an attorney, and asked me to make a poster for him called "How to be a Happy Lawyer." So, I created one as a gift for him, and as I sat there with my work, this is what materialized.

How to Be A HAPPY LAWYER

Quit

WHen you open the tiny Door, it sAys, "Quit"

I AM not AGAinst lawyers, it just seemed to me that the rest of the world WAS cAlling LArry. So He did Quit, For A Grand reason: A Full Fellowship AT UC Berkeley, For A MAster's Degree in Public policy. LArry HAS A Brilliant MinD and A very ARtistic, HumAnistic nature. He is HAppy and thriving in His new Life.

64

My FABULOUS AND VERY TRUE FRIEND Helen tells Her story: "I WAS WAITRESSING AND GETTING MY B.A. iN WOMEN'S STUDIES. THE WAITRESS WORK WASN'T FULFILLING MY PURPOSE ANYMORE, AND MY BODY BEGAN EXHIBITING UNHAPPY SYMPTOMS. So, the leap of FAITH WAS to KNOW I'D DO SOMETHING WONDERFUL, even iF I DIDN'T yet KNOW WHAT. I took MY WAITRESS SHOES, APRON AND LEATHER ORDER PAD ⁓ the "tools" I NEEDED to MAKE MONEY, AND TURNED THEM in to the GOODWILL." Helen's leaP oF FAITH leD Her to A MASTER'S DEGREE, AND BEING The EXECUTIVE DIRECTOR OF The San Francisco cHAPTER OF The nATIONAL ORGANIZATION for WOMEN, AND NOW, to WRITING, AND MAKING FiLMS. SHE SAYS, "SOMETIMES you JUST HAVE to PUT everyThiNG ASIDE AND HAVE FAiTH."

65

Live Juicy

flowers
to
GASP over

Living Juicy Means:
Rolling down a Bright Grassy Hill,
Sleeping All Day to stay in a Dream,
Definitely taking your shoes off at the
Beach, Dancing to your
Headphone stereo,
Buying Flowers that
Make you Gasp, Kissing
Puppies, running
Just For Fun, and
Imagining yourself
    M A G i C

I think it's possible to forget How
[ALive] we really Are.
We can Become Dry and tired, just
existing, instead of really Living.
We need to remind ourselves of the
juice of Life, and make that A
HABit.
Find those places inside
that jump For joy, and
Do things that Bring out
your Best, most magic
Self.
Keep Doing them!

J U M P
   For
   J   O   Y

Sometimes, iF I Become De·pressed,

it's usually because I need to express
something.
We all have paintings and music and
writing inside of us.
Keep supplies close
at hand: Brushes, pens,
Giant boxes of crayons,
Paints and pads of
Paper ~ the tools of
expression.
Make a letter writing
Box, and keep papers,
stamps, envelopes, pens
and an address book
inside.
Then, put it all aside and run outside
to say goodnight to the sun!

CRAYONS

My letter box
★ @ ...,☾

STAMP out conformity

One of my teachers of "Living Juicy" was definitely Miriam. She was 87 when she called to invite me to a Drawing class at her house.

"We're using a male model ~ but we'll have to draw fast ~ we don't want flaccid muscles!"

After class, we ate chocolate donuts the size of life preservers and sat by the fire, telling stories.

Live Juicy! Your aliveness will make the angels laugh.

69

Drive Away Fear

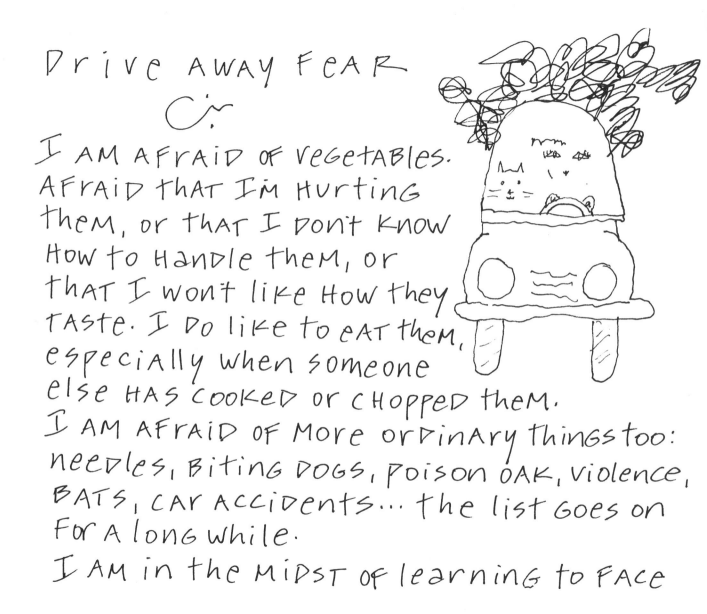

I AM AFRAID OF VEGETABLES. AFRAID THAT I'M HURTING THEM, or THAT I DON'T KNOW HOW TO HANDLE THEM, or THAT I won't like HOW they TASTE. I DO like to EAT them, especially when someone else HAS COOKED or CHOPPED THEM.

I AM AFRAID OF MORE ORDINARY things too: NEEDLES, BITING DOGS, POISON OAK, Violence, BATS, CAR ACCIDENTS... the list GOES on FOR A long while.

I AM in the MIDST OF learning to FACE

My FEARs. It seems that Fears Are All BASED on these things: illusion and Future thinking, with A side order of "WHAT iF." "WHAT iF that truck turns suddenly into our lane" "WHAT iF I'm All Alone AT AGe 80?"
WHAT iF? WHAT iF? WHAT iF?
Yes, FEARs must Be respected and learned ABout, But they must not PARAlyze us, or lure us into A HALF-LiFe oF Being AFRAID All the time. I like to think oF my FEARs Being Driven AWAy in A Rolls Royce (For it is true that once you FACE A FeAr, it loses All

of its stuffing, and will sit quietly in the BACK SEAT and DO AS it's TOLD.)

I FEEL THAT FEARS DRIVE US AWAY FROM our true selves as innocent BEINGS. I USED to live in DENIAL OF MY FEARS, and to try to cover them UP with A "HAPPY FACE."

I now see that MY GREATEST GROWTH is HAPPENING with an ACCEPTANCE OF MY FEARS, OF GIVING them voices, and learning new WAYS to DEAL with them.

THANK HEAVENS For therapy, SELF HEALING and GOD, HELPING ME to unRAVEL MY FEARS, BECAUSE it's A Process I'M AFRAID to DO Alone!

HAVE WILD IMAGININGS,
Transformative Dreams and perfect CALM

One of my favorite games to play in
my journal is called: I want. I write
"I want" and then let wild imaginings
make things up. Here is an example
from my journal:
I want to write a book about miracles.
I want to see a baby buffalo. I
want red rubber rainboots. I want
to eat butterscotch pudding at
midnight. I want twin baby turtles,
a new walking stick and clean white
socks. I want to change the

School system in America. I want to practice on a trapeze, wear new corduroy pants and have a new friend who's old.

Transformative dreams await us each time we sleep. I like to ask questions before sleeping, and then dream the answers.

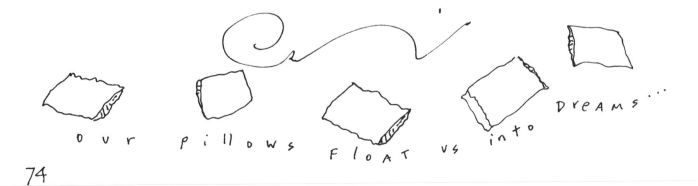

our   pillows   FLOAT   us   into   DREAMS...

Dreams love to guide us and answer questions we're not ready to ask our conscious mind. I do write down all my dreams, and now have hundreds of dreams in my journals to reread for clues to my unconscious.

Dreams are the angels of our spirits.

our spirits will guide us if we listen

Perfect CALM seems to come to me in moments.

That first sip of tea.
Watching a spider spin.
First moments of rainfall.
Tucking into bed with clean sheets, just after the light is turned off.

Watch for perfect CALM. I think it loves attention. I am presently trying to learn more about perfect CALM by meditating. So far, I've meditated once. I've spent a lot of time in extreme moods, and perfect CALM is very new to me. You can think of me, learning to let perfect CALM happen!

plant impossible GARDens

I love it when people say, "you can't
do that."
It's like HEARING "I DARE you."
When I went to europe Alone AT AGE 19,
these same people said, "switzerland
is very expensive, you can't expect to
Live there."
So of course, I went to switzerland
immediately, and met a man in Zermatt,
looking for a housesitter for His chalet
that HAD just been built into the side
of a mountain, Accessible only by

CHAIRLIFT.

YEARS AGO, in the BAHAMAS, I
HAD no MONEY, and WAS tired
OF sleeping in the lounge CHAIRS
By the pool. I went to one OF
the BiG Hotels and Asked to see
the Manager. I told Him that I WOULD
like to BABysit or teACH swimming
in exchange For A rooM.
He just looked AT Me, and then reACHED
into A DrAwer, took out A set OF Keys
and pusHED them Across the DESK.
"TAke these. I WAS youn G AND Broke
once too."

The keys opened the door to a penthouse on the top floor. I lived there for a month.

I like to take the impossibles and make them possible.

I believe that we need to GO TO where we want to be, and the resources will follow us.

IMPOSSIBLE means I'M POSSIBLE!

Plant all your impossible gardens, and see WHAT BLOOMS!

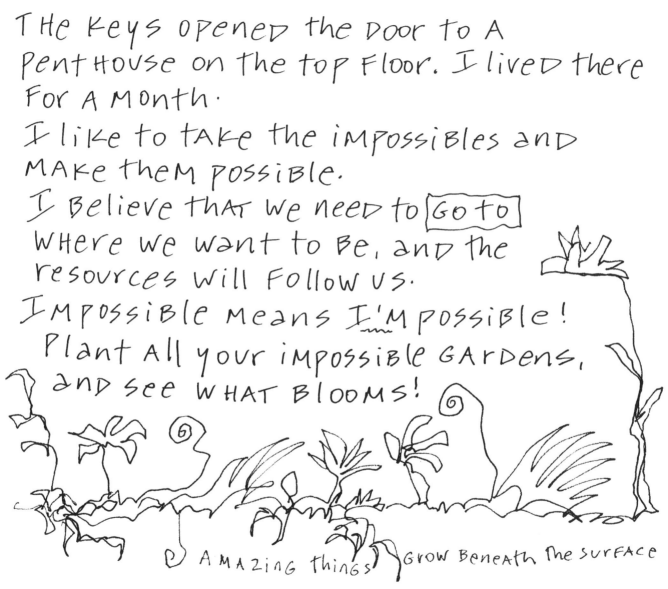

AMAZING things grow beneath the surface

Write your own books!
(keep a journal)

AMAZING stories of mine

nobody else can write what you write. nobody.

FiND your own voice! Then, let it Be HeArD All over the world

WHen I WAS 26 yeArs OLD, I HAD to FinD oUt ABoUT MyseLF, anD whether or noT I WAS "reAlly" A writer. I'D spent A lot oF time living wiLDly, anD HAVinG All Sorts oF ADventures, with very little time for reflection vpon those experiences.

I FOUND MyseLF BACK in Minnesota, Sitting in the little pLAyHouse tHAt My GranDFather, "BoppA" HAD BUiLt For Me, anD Where I HAD written My First

BOOK AT AGE 10. I HAD A STACK OF
SCHOOL COMPOSITION NOTEBOOKS, AND
I BEGAN WRITING EVERYDAY.

My own writing
BORED ME, BUT I TRIED
to iGnore THAT.

I reAD everyone's JOURNALS: anais nin,
MAY SARton and so many others. I reAD
All of Henry Miller, and every BOOK
Written ABout JOURNAL Keeping.

THE MESSAGE FROM All these writings
WAS CLEAR: "Keep Writing."

So, I DECIDED to Keep Writing
NO MATTER WHAT. It worKeD.

By the eArLy 1980's, I'D BeGun

To Feel confined in my lined composition notebooks, and BOUGHT A BiG BlAcK BoUND JOURNAL/sKetchBook, and A Box OF crAyolA MArkers to go with it.
By now, I HAD MOVED to San Francisco and WAs living in the Victorian Hotel OF ARTS and MUSiC.
My writing exPANDED in many WAys After thAT. I wrote in All Different Colors, Quite lArGe. As L A r G e AS I Felt like.
It DeliGhteD Me to see those BiG Color·Full Books eMerGe.
Now, I HAve over 100 oF them.

Since 1989, My JouRNALS ARe SMALLeR
in size, anD I print Quite SMALL,
BecAuse now thAt Delights Me.
My JOURNALS HAppen to Be written
with an eye towARDS SHARING theM
with others SOMeDAY. My wonDeR·FuLl
FrienD ADrienne HAS BeGun reADING
theM. So FAR, SHe HAS reAD 10. I
love Her iMMersion in My JournAL WORLD.
    I love JOURNAL Keeping BecAuse
it HeLpeD Me to Discover anD uncover
MYseLF, to en·courAGe My own BRAVery,
Sort out My DiFFicuLties with other
People, to invent new wAys OF BeinG,

and of seeing, to plan All Kinds of Adventures and plans, and Most of All, to live experiences more than once.

. Twice in the writing, three times in the reading.

I once read that the writer erica Jong traveled with All Her Finished and unfinished Manuscripts in a suitcase, and showed them to no one. Because then she could Be judged.

HAving judged Myself For years, I can relate to that. I found out that I AM indeed, A writer and an Artist, and that I HAve A lot to sHAre with others.

My journals are dear friends, and very creative companions. They are a holder of my dreams, a celebration of moments, a collection of miracles, and a joy to have created.
Write your books. The ones that [only you] can tell.

We all support you!

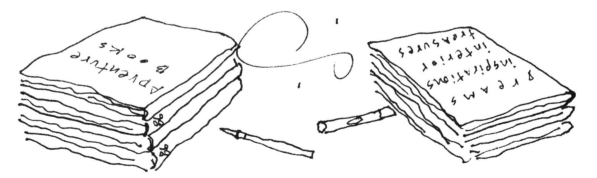

How to Go out Alone
(and have a fabulous time)

People frequently say to me,
"you went there Alone? I
could never do that."

Oh yes, you could!
Pick 3 places that have
fascinated you in some way, and let's
plan to go there.
Here is the "equipment" I need for a
time out with myself.

1. A good book
2. notebook, sketchbook
3. tiny set of paints
4. change for the phone
5. feeling safe

I'm Actually A SHy person, so I can offer HELPFUL WAys to set sHyness Aside.

I Dress in something that Delights me.

I pretend to Be looking For someone.

I Go to the pHone and call A Dear Friend, to Feel Grounded.

I Definitely tALK to strangers.

I set up my "CAMP" with A cup oF teA, A smAll snAck, A Good seAt and my sketch Book and watercolors (which I might not Actually use.)

I MAke Friends with the service person.

reMINDer: THis is the Best time to
MAKe use oF the AFFirMAtion:
"I AM welcome everyWHere."
I settle in, and Do some people WATCHING/
OBserving, MAKinG up Stories ABout
some of the people I see.
Sometimes, I write A note to someone
WHo interests Me, inviting them to
HAve teA.
reMeMBer: A place is lucky to HAve
[You] visit it!

I enJoy My own CoMpany, lAUGH At
MyseLF, anD KNow thAT MAny ADventures
Can HAppen WHen we're willing to
traveL Alone.

Then, your 3 places can become familiar to you, and you can look forward to "dates" with yourself.
Here is a drawing I did on one of my "self dates."

1. While I waited for the Bittersweet Chocolate Obsession dessert to arrive, the bread became an alligator!

2. Then there appeared an enormous chocolate pod, complete with chocolate bowling balls!

in celebration of Deep night

"The air is filled with the dreams of the sleeping people."

I am usually awake from midnight until 7 am. It's a rich creative time for me. There aren't any distractions, interruptions, or "things to do" in the outside world.

There is a certain penetrating kind of quiet at night.

My pen leaps to paper, paints and bits of colored paper are scattered across the floor.

I shuffle around wearing incredibly wrinkled and well-loved PAJAMAS, robes, sweatshirts and thick socks. All sorts of new ideas bloom in the night. The night time is like special soil for creative gardens. Usually music accompanies me, and special kinds of incense, and carefully chosen lighting. I measure time by mugs of tea

Being nocturnal is a curious thing in a world that promotes the 9-5 life. I make no appointments until after 3pm, and sometimes people find this odd. (not as odd as I find 9 am!)

Many times, I AM Blessed to see Both sunrise and sunset. I Find it is imperative to Feel As Free As possible About sleeping. I cannot "Go to sleep early" the night Before, to prepare For some Activity or event the next DAY.

I claim as much Freedom As possible For my sleeping HABits.

I recently read About some sleep research that WAS Done. The suBject took naps whenever He WAS tired, and Did As He liked. He took 10 naps A DAY, and never needed to sleep more than A Few Hours Altogether. They called this "Multiple napping."

I support people taking naps and simply staying in bed whenever the urge is there.

Someday, we will have "nap rooms" in stores, restaurants and airports. Think how grand it will be!

If you have any inclinations to stay up all night, do it. Arrange your life to accommodate your best sleeping style.

Why daylight savings time? Why not night-time spending time?

nap rooms with beds like cool pockets... places to slip into and slide into a dream...

~ Q u o t e s ~

"DREAMS DON'T
COME true ~
DREAMS ARE TRUE"
RUBY Montana

"So you see, iMAGinAtion
NEEDS MOODLING — LONG,
inefficient, HAPPY iDLinG,
DAWDLinG anD puttering."
BrenDA VeLanD

"Why Does anyBoDy
reAD or write A Book?
IF I wanteD to SEARCH
For truth, I couLD FinD
it in story. Story can
TAke us FAr, FAr Beyond
FACT."

MADeleine L'enGle

"Be Always ecstAstic.
Be FilleD with A
Divine intoxicAtion."
Henry Miller

"Whoever uses The spirit
thAt is in Him creAtively
is an ARtist. To MAke
living itself an ARt,
thAt is The GoAL."
Henry Miller

94

"To walk in money through the night crowd, protected by money, lulled by money, dulled by money, the crowd itself a money, the breath money, no least single object anywhere that is not money. Money, money everywhere and still not enough! and then no money, or a little money, or less money, or more money but money always money. and if you have money, or you don't have money it is the money that counts, and money makes money, but what makes money make money?"

By Henry Miller
From: Money and How it Gets that Way

"From now on I hope always to stay alert, to educate myself as best I can. But lacking this, in future I will relaxedly turn back to my secret mind to see what it has observed when I thought I was sitting this one out. We never sit anything out.
We are cups, constantly and quietly being filled. The trick is, knowing how to tip ourselves over and let the beautiful stuff out."

Ray Bradbury

People sharing at a creativity gathering with SARK, June 1992

"Regarding the "dark side" and creativity: I don't like to think of it as that—I like to think of sunlight and shade..."

"The Brightest sunlight produces the Darkest shadows..."

Q: Any suggestions about showing my work? I'm shy and don't let it out much.

A: Choose kind people to see it. People who will be gentle with you and your fragile, new discoveries. So often, we start from a place of scarcity or low self esteem, and choose a critical person to look at our work. Don't do it!

"I was in a group, with about 30 people, and when we started, I didn't think any of them were very creative. By the middle, I had seen that they were more creative than I could have ever imagined!"

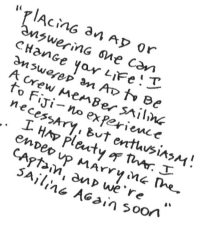

"Placing an ad or answering one can change your life! I answered an ad to be a crew member sailing to Fiji—no experience necessary, but enthusiasm! I had plenty of that. I ended up marrying the captain, and we're sailing again soon"

Q: How can I help my child keep his/her creativity alive?

A: By nourishing your own creative spirit. Draw on the walls! Eat cake with no hands! Keep the gleam in your own eye—your children will absorb it like plants.

Live your AFFiRMATions

One of the wonder. Full ways to be inspired is through the use of AFFiRMATions. It is Also A powerful tool for transforming negative "self talk."

Thanks to Louise Hay, H.J. Kramer, Julie evans, and my ever growing spiritual family for teaching and sharing AFFiRMations. ♡

I created a small book called <u>Daily Miracles</u>, which I AM reproducing Here for you to remove, Add your own ART or photos, and use to remind you that

You Are Already A Miracle

Guide to Assembling Your Book

Cr̃?

You will be adding images to 7 of the pages.

Cut out images from magazines, or old photographs, or draw and paint your own.

Find or create images for these affirmations:

1. There are miracles everywhere 2. relax
3. Fill your heart with wonder 4. you are not alone 5. Have an adventure 6. Hug a tree
7. relax (the pages are perforated! it's easy)

Remove your <u>Daily Miracles</u> book, and each page with a circle in the top left hand corner may be punched, and yarn or string threaded to connect the pages.

O

DAiLY

MirAcles

There Are miracles everywhere

o

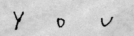

You

Are

an

inspiration

relax

YOU ARE enough

YOU HAVE enough

YOU DO enough

Fill your HEART with wonder

O

YOU
BRING
LAUGHTER
TO SO MANY
HEARTS

y o u   A r e   n o t   A l o n e

H A v e   a n   A d v e n t u r e

HvG A Tree

relax

THis BooK HAS BeeN created with love and joy!

Yes!

Transform Negatives

I started out with a gigantic negative.
I'm a survivor of sibling incest.
After years of healing and recovery,
I announced to my therapist,
"I just figured out the positive side to the abuse!"

She looked stunned, and curious.
I went on.

"During those years of abuse, I retreated into my imagination and just lived there. It made me intensely creative."

It was the one gleaming star in the midst of the horror.

I wish more than anything that I had never been molested, but since it happened, I needed to try and find a way of transforming that kind of awesome negativity.

It helps me to reclaim some of what was lost.

I would also like to honor all the victims and survivors that don't find one single positive thing about their being abused! It was just my way to transform some of that negativity. My creativity was a way for me to express myself, and open some of the doors that had slammed shut.

I AM still HEALING, AND HAVE BEGUN
DOING inner CHILD WORK to HELP All
the WOUNDED CHILDREN inside ME.

THis is the First TIME I HAVE written
PUBLicly ABout the incest, AND I KNOW
thAT it can only HELP to HEAL MYSELF,
AND All the SHAMED, Silent voices thAT
MAY BE AFrAID to SPEAK. My only GOAL
is HEALING.

I Believe thAT we can use the pain to
trans·Form AND Give new Form to the
DeePest, MoST DAMAGED PArts of our
Selves.

One of the many books to help me tremendously is called The Courage to Heal By Ellen Bass and Laura Davis.

My Boyfriend at the time wouldn't read the chapter called "For Partners" and I got angry after asking many times. One night, I just ripped the entire chapter out of the book and handed it to him.

"Here! Take it home and read it!"

A year or so later, Laura Davis wrote a book called The Courage to Heal Workbook. I stood in a Bookstore, looking at it, to decide

IF I WOULD BUY it. I WAS Feeling
WEAry OF All this HEAling work, and
HOPED I COULD escape this workbook.
Finally, I ASKED GOD For A "sign" and
OpeneD the BOOK with my eyes cloSED.
   THe PAGE and PARAGRAPH I turneD to
WAS my very own story of ripping the
CHApter out of the BooK to Hand to my
Boyfriend! I HAD CALLED LAUrA DAVis
JuSt AFter it HAppeneD, to tell Her About
it, and SHe HAD USED my story in Her
WorKBOOK!

I BOUGHT the workBOOK.

Autobiography in Five Short Chapters

By Portia Nelson

I

I walk down the street.
  There is a deep hole in the sidewalk.
  I fall in
  I am lost... I am helpless
        It isn't my fault.
It takes forever to find a way out.

II

I walk down the same street
  There is a deep hole in the sidewalk.
  I pretend I don't see it.
  I fall in again.
I can't believe I am in the same place.
    But it isn't my fault.
It still takes a long time to get out.

III

I walk down the same street
  There is a deep hole in the sidewalk
  I see it is there.
  I still fall in... it's a habit.
      My eyes are open
        I know where I am
  It is my fault.
  I get out immediately.

IV

I walk down the
  same street.
  There is a deep hole
  in the sidewalk.
  I walk around it.

V

I walk down another
street.

Write more letters!

A BOOK is like A BiG letter to
the WORLD. Letters Are More ways
to sHare our spirits.
I reMeMBer Writing to MAy Sarton,
the Author, and receiving the Most
enDEAring and Friendly letter in
reply, and How MucH it WARMeD Me.

DEAr SARK
WHAT A DEAr
letter you sent
to me! I thee-

SARK

I'M AstonisHeD By the
MAGic of letters: thin pAper trAveling
Many or Few miles, propelleD only

By words and a tiny glued stamp.
Kiss your mailperson!

I believe in keeping this ART OF
letter writing ALive and thriving.
Letters Are truly presents for our SOULS.

Here Are some of my FAvorite excerpts
From letters I've received in response
to my FIRST BOOK, A Creative Companion.
"I WAS transported to A WORLD WHere
A person COULD HUG trees, WATCH snails,
and tAKe nAps whenever they wanted.
You Are the First true creative spirit
I've ever known. I've Always HAD A

GOOD iMAGinAtion, especiAlly when I was younger, But lately I Feel like I've Become too serious. I don't want to Be norMAL or orDinary! I just want to Be Free to Be Myself.
P.S. I'm only 15, so I'm not too serious yet."

"I MADE A COMMitMent to Honor My creAtive spirit, But sometimes I HeAr this voice thAt tells me I'm not Being "responsiBle." THis is why I needed to see your inspiring Book. It's such A confirMAtion to know thAt there Are other creAtive spirits such As you, Living their Life in the liGHt, and

I'M not Alone or Crazy. THanks so MUCH For Giving the Free spirits of the world A lovely, wonderful and spiritual Gift-yourself."

"I curled up in Bed to reAD your Book As you suggested, even though it was noon and most would say "Why Are you still in Bed? (including My DAD ~ He's 46 and Doesn't Know How to relax—MAYBe I'll MAKe Him reAD The Book!""

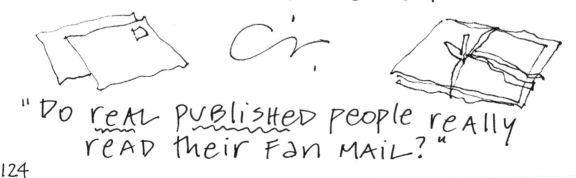

"Do reAL PUBLisHeD people reAlly reAD their FAn MAiL?"

Oh yes, Definitely! I reAD anD treasure All MAiL.

"I love your BooK. Whenever I open its pAGes, it's like BeGinning to Breathe AGain After HOLDinG your BreAth for A lonG time. everything ABout the Book speAKs to Me. I love the colors, your printing anD the precious, encourAGinG, Life renewinG and life reMinDinG worDs. THanKs so MUCH! My journey towArD A creAtive, joy FilleD life continues..."

"Dear SARK~ Alas, no missive, papyrus, illuminated manuscript, book of hours or any communication sent by a citizen of the earth, could equal that magnificent burst of colour, exuberance and joy, as your letter was to me."

MiriAM WornuM

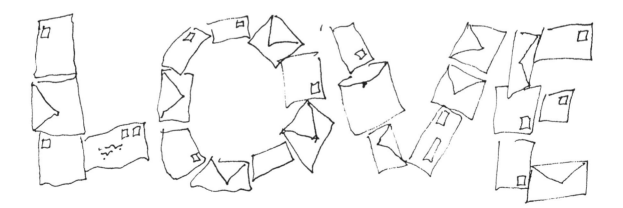

DRAW on the WALLS

I Believe we neeD to MAKe More use of the wALls we live with. often, they're white canvasses. just wAitinG For us to paint theM! When I WAS creatinG the cover for My First BOOK, I HAD A DreAM DurinG A nAP OF HOW it WOULD looK. I woKe up anD Drew it on the wAll with pasteL cHALK. It's still there. THe only proBleM is thAt My CAT Jupiter ruBs AGainsT it andGeTs pasteL stripes on His BLACK Fur! Write the worD [Yes] on your wALls.

Paint raspberry stripes in the kitchen!

There is a wonderful bright plastic paint called Tulip, that comes in little squeeze bottles. I use it to paint my tennis shoes, and sometimes, chairs. Actually, I paint whatever needs new life.

People have described my tennis shoes as "Melted Jelly Beans" or "psychedelic pizza". Whenever the paint looks weary, I just add more. So far, there are about a dozen layers. They're "Happy shoes" because they make people smile.

ABOUT MY 250 JOBS...

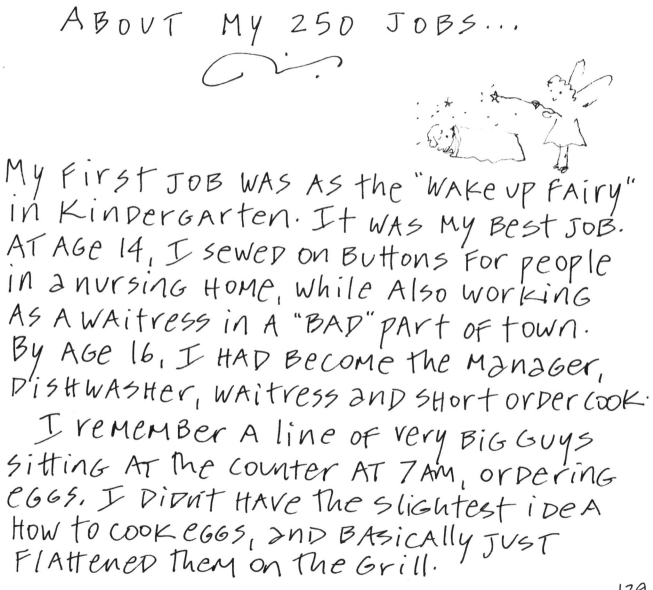

My First JOB WAS AS the "WAKE UP FAiry" in KinDerGArten. It WAS MY BeSt JOB. AT AGe 14, I seweD on Buttons For people in a nursing HOMe, while Also working AS A WAitress in A "BAD" pArt of town. By AGe 16, I HAD BecoMe the Manager, DiSHWASHer, WAitress anD SHort orDer cook.

   I reMeMBer A line of very BiG Guys Sitting AT the counter AT 7AM, orDering eGGS. I DiDnt HAve the slightest iDeA How to cook eGGS, anD BASiCAlly JUST FlAtteneD theM on the Grill.

Then, I WOULD Deliver
the plate, and run to
the other end of The
Counter.

"You, GirL! THese Arent sunnyside up! I
ordered sunnyside up!"
I WOULD turn and SAY, with My Hands
on My Hips,
"They're eggs Arent they? eAT 'em!"
All the other Guys WOULD roAr lAugHing,
and leAve Big tips.
    One summer, I Got A Job putting
ruBber tips on DARTs thAT shoot out of
toy Guns. every Few Hours, A Furious
FACeD WOMan WOULD APPeAr to weigH
My BAG and tell Me to work FAster.

I used to deliberately squirt glue in my eye, so I could go to the infirmary and lie down.

I saw darts in my sleep!

For years, I sold vacuum cleaners and washing machines in a department store. I was finally asked to leave when the store manager asked if I was wearing a bra, while leering at me. I asked if he was wearing a jock strap!

Then, there was the summer I taught archery at a girl's camp. The only problem was, I'd never used a bow, or shot an arrow. I checked out all the books on archery in the

Library, and went there, bluffing.

The Archery class was at 9 AM, with 30 whining 9 year old girls who HATED Archery. By 9:30, it was already 90°, and Horseflies began landing on my head, biting. Somehow, I hit a few bulls-eyes and managed to twang the string on the inside of my forearm, blackening it from wrist to elbow.

Strangely enough, it was thought that only a "real expert" would do that, and I didn't get to escape teaching Archery!

When I worked as a hat check person, I used to put $10 and $20 dollar bills in my tip basket, and bet people to double my money if I could make them laugh. While they laughed, I tried finding their coats, which were unreasonably heavy and all looked identical.

Being a waitress always filled in any job gaps. Now, I always overtip in restaurants. Countless "temporary" jobs came and went, and I remember frantic hours at new switchboards in offices, disconnecting everyone.

Most of my sales jobs involved "Demonstrating" the product, and I Demonstrated calculators, Blenders, crepe makers, coffee machines, Hair Dryers, Food processors, scissors, Popcorn makers and Photo albums... yes, photo albums!

I would stand in a store aisle, with a photo album full of fake family pictures, "your family photos could be here."

I remember wearing a 75 pound sandwich board and mask, handing out coupons. Mercifully, I Dont recall what it was for. Obviously I survived all my jobs, and they all

HELPED to FORtiFY MY DeterminAtion to Do something else... anything else!

I've Been "SeLF employeD" As A writer anD ARtist For 14 yeArs, anD it's true thAt MY pAYCHeCKS were non-existent For A long time, Bvt I continveD to creAte. IM the toughest Boss I know, anD Also the Best. One oF MY Best JOB BeneFits is unliMiteD nAps anD weAring PAJAMAS As work clothes.

I Believe thAt there's room For every person to work At A JOB they love, anD we need to MAGnify thAt BelieF in our society.

MAKe your work your DreAM, or
Be sure it leADs to your DreAM.
IF it Doesn't Do either of these,
Quit sooner rAther than later.

Yes,
you can!

MAKe little signs that say [Yes] and post them
All over your House.

Yes. It is A power. Full word. Yes can Affect
us subliminally, even when we're not
concentrating on it. Yes can move us in
Fascinating directions and trans.Form our
thoughts. I made this sign For you!

Y e s

Don't you love when they draw these little scissors?

137

Be WHo you Are and the Money
will Follow

There were DAys I Ate ketcHUp
SAnDwicHes. I used to look in My
refrigerAtor anD SAY
"WHo lives Here? WHy Don't they BUY
FOoD?"
I WAS DRAWING, WritinG, struGGLinG,
LivinG Life. I tHouGHT I HAD to pAY
For HAppiness BY HAVinG no Money!
I now know thAt isn't true.
People SAY "Do WHAT you Love anD the
Money will Follow." I think it HELpS
To unDerstanD thAt we MUST Be

HOW TO relax ABOUT MONEY

relax. Your money is not your Life!
it just seems that way sometimes.
True wealth is inside of you. learn to
cultivate money miracles. Go BACK TO
MONEY innocence. Be who you truly Are
and the money will follow. You Are SAFE.
if you find yourself worrying About Money,
why were you lost in the first place? read
"money and How it gets that way" by Henry
Miller. MAKE friends with money. MONEY
is like love- the more you give Away, the more
comes BACK. WATCH the MOVIE "it's A wonderful life." When any money flows in for
you, it's time to Help others. Help them
now. Money was invented to be SHARED.
START A revolution: refuse to believe
in recessions. We need to rewrite
recession to read: Money recess.
remember recess? You got to go outside, kick A BALL, and feel free from
school. We All need to feel free ABOUT
MONEY! TAKE A deep BReATH.
WHAT you Are worth is not ABOUT Money.
relax. YOU Are SAFE

©SARK'21

Being A WonderFull Friend

Open your ♥ wide. let your HeArt leAD the WAY. Follow your in sights. extend surprising invitations. reAD the SAME BOOKS. SereNADe eAch other. write A poem on the siDewALK with coloreD CHALK. MAKe A BOOK of your FrienDShip MeMories. HAVe A privAte DAnce recitAL AT A PArK. MAKe A pAPer DoLL of your FrienD, with clothes. WASH eAch other's HAir. HAVe A picnic with only Desserts. MAKe A DiorAMA in A Shoe Box. Give SMALL treAsures FounD in nAture. recite poetry in tanDeM. Go For A Moonlight HiKe. if there is anger, wAit until one of you Forgets, then cALL and SAY, "Do you want to play?" SHAre feelings SAFely. plan A FrienDShip rituAL together. SenD enDeAring letters. Be willing to Be sepArAte. leArn to ForGive eAch other. HAVe A teA PArty: weAr HATS and eAt plenty of cookies. cultivate compAssion. Sit in the sun together and lAugh. plAn the next FIFty yeArs of your FrienDShip. Be your own "Best" FrienD. A PAir of frienDs is likely to Do anything!

WHO we truly Are, to DO WHAT WE love.

For many years, I HAD known I WAS A writer anD ARtist, anD wAsn't Doing it, or Being it. InsteAD, I HAD 250 JOBS to "PAy the Bills." THe ProBleM WAS THAT my writing anD ARt GOT lost in the MiDDle OF All those JOBS.

THen, I "StArveD" For yeArs WHile I WAS ActvAlly Doing My ART.

THere is A MiDDle route Between these 2 extremes, anD I'M still learning ABout it.

Many people HeLPeD Me During the yeArs oF ketcHUp SanDwicHes, anD the Author Henry Miller WAS one.

It helped me so much to read that He would go outside, throw his arms in the air and say "I owe everyone!" He also figured out a plan to have Dinner at a different friend's house every night— it worked! Much of His writing supports the idea of creating Despite poverty, and especially, creating-no-matter-what.

Another person to help me tremendously is named David. While I lived at the Victorian Hotel of Arts and Music, trading Art for rent, He sent money for food and stamps and library fines. Most of all, He believed in me, and supported that belief with money for Many years. That Helped give

Me the faith to continue creating.

My dear friend Helen was the first person to commission a piece of my art, and then pay me for it from her job as a waitress. My list of gratitude is long, and I give thanks every day.

Do your art (whatever it may be)
Find a believer/supporter (or several)
Trade and barter (especially for rent)
Pay close attention to the miracles
Follow the path of your dream
Wherever it may lead!

Give Money Away

cir

There are many ways to give money away. Using your creativity to help others is a fabulous way. (It is a way to circulate good energy.)

I created a poster to advertise a book sale to benefit the library, and they raised a record amount of money.

If you have a friend in transition, or worried about money, mail them some anonymously. cir Find places that need your energy and give some away. cir

We think that money is limited, but it is truly unlimited, and can expand according to our prayers and beliefs.

iMAGine yourseLF MAGic

I remember riding
My Bicycle when it
could Still Be A Horse.
I'd PACK some kind of
lunch and ride until
My "Horse" and I were
tired. Sometimes, the
territory seemed rough
and FAr AWAY From Home, But thAt Helped ADD
to the MAGic.
Sometimes, while reADING A BOOK sitting in the
leAFy seAT of My Apple tree in the BACKYArD,
I could DisAPPeAr into the PAGes and Become
the Pippi LongStocking thAt I knew lived

inside me. I can still capture that magic today, and plan to live that way always.

It helps to spend time with children because their vision of magic is so clear. A few years ago, I made treasure maps, and hid them under bricks in my garden.

Now, those maps are "mysteriously" gone, and I imagine the answer is... MAGIC!

Live your Adventures!

At age 20, I wanted to live in Paris. While on a train in Switzerland, a man told me to go to a bookstore called Shakespeare & Co.

"Tell George that Bob referred you." I found the bookstore, across from the Notre Dame Cathedral, and the man called George was eating a whole Sara Lee cake out of the tin with his fingers. When I said that Bob had sent me, he paused for a moment, with crumbs falling to the floor.

"Well, then! Hurry upstairs to the rare library and serve tea and gingerbread! Hurry along!"

I climbed some steep and crooked stairs, and found the rare library. There was gingerbread steaming on a breadboard, and people sitting in rocking chairs, waiting to be served.

After tea, I came downstairs, and George thrust a cigar box full of French money into my hands.

"Here! This is the money box. Take care of the store for an hour or so while I go out."

I didn't speak a word of French, and had to trust people to give and take correct change.

Boit D'Argent

Argent

The "hour or so" stretched into the rest of the afternoon.

George said that I could live at the bookstore in exchange for helping with the books.

My bed was up a ladder, behind a purple velvet curtain, in a nook between the book-shelves. A poster on the wall across from my bed proclaimed

T	O		
L	i	v	e	H e r e
	Y	o	u
M	U	S	T
	r	e	A	D
A	B O O K	A	D A Y

149

It was a perfect place for me. Books balanced in impossibly precarious stacks. Tiny, narrow rows had been made to walk through the piles. Thick dust held the place together, and it vibrated with literary History.

I soon found out that George rarely remembered my name, or whether I had helped out or not. So sometimes, I spent my time exploring Paris...

I think I was an "adventure specialist" for a long time.

WHATever place FASCinATeD Me, I
went there. My youthful exuberance
CArried Me in anD ouT oF Many
Precarious anD tantALyZinG SituATions.

I Do recoMMenD ADventures.
   HAve As Many As possiBle.
StuFF your experiences into All
your cells anD truly:

L   i   v   e   y   o   u   r   ADventures

Find inspiring people

Inspiring people Are vitAmins for our spirits. THey come in All kinds of Disguises anD Descriptions. IF you open your HeArT to BeinG inspireD, they will AppeAr.

One oF my FAvorite endlessly inspiring People WAS MiriAM. SHe toLD me this story ABout BeinG younG in the 1900's anD traveling Around the worLD with Her parents. "I woulD Be in

Singapore or some such place with my parents, and my sister and I would just stay in bed reading. My mother would come in and say, "Get off your filthy mattresses and see the temple of a thousand steps!"

But we wouldn't budge. Late at night, after our parents were asleep, my sister and I would sneak out, and hire a rickshaw to drive us to the red light districts and see things they never dreamed of! I would carry a scimitar in my lap ~ I had no idea how to use the thing ~ I just carried it to look threatening!"

153

Inspiring people help us to experience life in a new way.

The delight moves us.

Another inspirational woman is the poet Maya Angelou. She beams inspiration. Her voice fills a well way inside me. When I heard her speak before an audience, she absolutely filled the auditorium with her incandescent presence.

In the darkness, you could see every heart leaping out to greet her, glowing. Her songs, words and poetry made ecstatic melodies for us to hear.

MADeleine L'enGle, the Author, tells stories and weAves All the spirits in the room together.

Cゔ

Author, speAker RAM DASS, speAks like A root Beer FLOAT: Fizzy, FAmiliar and refresHinG.

Cゔ

All oF my FrienDs inspire me too. I Believe thAT inspiration can illuminAte tiny pArts oF ourselves and Help them to Grow.

When we speAk oF A DreAm, or creAtive iDeA, an inspirational FrienD can

Help give it the juice to take shape.

How can you tell if a friend is inspiring?

After spending time together, you will feel lighter, happier and bursting with some kind of new energy.

It can be quiet energy, and it may not reveal itself until later, but you will begin to recognize the feel of inspiration.

Then you can expand upon it, search it out, spend time there.

Bask in the light of inspiration. Soak up the slanted rays of its energy.

Once we begin to spend time with inspiring people, we will become more inspiring ourselves.

It will stick to us.

I wish you absolute inspiration.

it's rare

it's free

and makes us full

Most of All, inspire your self!

Find a tree, and sit at it's roots
and listen

Pick up a rock, and Hear it speak

The Moon is our nightlight,
The sun our everglow...

The world will turn eagerly
towards you to Hear your inspiring

Words and songs, see your paintings and drawings, touch your sculptures, drink your films and embrace all your inspiration!

Let your inspiration feed others, and give them the juice to grow, and to glow.

See you in dreams, and telepathic communication, and perhaps at a picnic for inspired souls, or in a city of angels...

Bless you,
SARK
Valentine's Day
Magic Cottage
San Francisco 1992

Write to me! Send me
something inspiring...

By
First
Class
Miracles

PUT
STAMP
upside
down

From
your
House

SARK
CAMP SARK
PO BOX 330039
SAN FRANCISCO, CA
USA   94133

To
mine

From my inside child to yours

More WAYS To Be involved

To order BOOKS : posters : CAll 1·800·841·BOOK, or write to
Celestial ARTS (c/o order Dept.) PO Box 7327, Berkeley CA 94707

BOOKS:

THE Cottage Book

MAGIC APPress $16.95

Living Daily Morsels For creative

JUICY Morsels your Soul $15.95

inspiration sandwich Stories To inspire our creative freedom $14.95

Or ASK your LocAL BookStore To order SARK Books For you They'll Arrive in Just A Few DAYS. support Bookstores : libraries

SARK's and PLAY! A place While Awake

JournAL BooK To DreAm $19.95

A creative How To Free your spirit

Companion to creative 12.95

AUDIO TApe

A creative Companion Audio Tape reAd by SARK 10.95

SARK rides A creative cycle

To order Audio TApes of
<u>A Creative Companion</u> And
<u>Succulent Wild Woman</u>
CAll: Audio LiterAture
At 1-800-383-0174

posters

HOW TO BE an ARTIST
Full size 3.95
23 x 35
Demi 3.50
14¾ x 22½

Just For Mom
Full size 23 x 32 4.95
Demi 3.50
14¾ x 20

To order copies of
<u>Succulent Wild Woman</u> or
<u>The Bodacious Book of Succulence</u>
And other Simon & Schuster titles
CAll 1·800·223·2336
e-MAil: CAMPSARK@Best.COM
Please visit us on the web!
WWW.CAMPSARK.COM
For generAl informAtion And A peek into
SARK's creAtive schedule, CAll
415·397·SARK (7275) '24 Hrs. A dAy)

CAll:

The inspiration Line
415-546-epic (3742)
A 3-5 minute recorded
message by SARK
A Wonder·Full place
to give or receive
inspiration 24 hours A dAy!

Visit SARK At
WWW.CAMPSARK.COM

More Good Stuff

The Henry Miller Library
Highway One (1/4 mile south of nepenthe)
Big Sur CA 93920
408·667·2574
Open to the public
Open every day except Monday during summer
Call for off season hours

A fascinating collection of Henry Miller and friends in a redwood grove. You will be welcomed here. Call or write the library for membership information or to find out more about Henry Miller books.

Your public library is full of good stuff. Go there. Help them.

The Success Hotline by Dr. Rob Gilbert
A treasury of motivation and inspiration
201·743·4690
Message changes daily
24 hrs.

THE Transformation GAME
Available in stores or call the creators
704·665·9937
PO Box 10502 Asheville, NC 28806
A Game about the way you play your life
WHAT A WONDEROUS GAME

Yes! SARK is writing more books...

Books ♡ love these people and I deeply thank them ♡

PHIL WOOD

DAVID HINDS

JO ANN DECK

SAL GLYNN

Special thanks to: Peggy Millin "angel editor"

There is a great tribe of Dearhearts at Celestial Arts and I thank: Marie ♡ George ♡ Sheri ♡ Rachel ♡ Nancy ♡ Nicole ♡ Brook ♡ Torri ♡ Leili ♡ Maureen ♡ Steve

THaNKs TO: • lOvE BuBBles over • PlAyHOuse PARADise IsLAND MinneApolis WHite BeAr LAKe NeW York CiTY TeLeGRAPH Hill SAN FRANcisco MARTiNique THe cAFe AND ALWAys JAMAicA BiG SuR MinneHAHA cReeK FiLbeRT steps

"loVe's MAJesty"
AdRienne ♡ Ken
"the continUAl UnFolDING of loVe"

MiRiAM WORNUM ♡
"My DeAR FRiend
and Mentor"

TO My GRAND PARents WHO WeRe there in the BeGinninG ♡

♡ RoBert BReweR HAMILton YounG
"ancient angel"

WHAT A FABULoUs GUy!
♡ My BRother
andReW
"WHo tells Me truths"

NANeW ♡ MARcus
"angel twins"

GOD
"WHo is AlL·WAys
RiGHT in The MiDst
of eveRything·
(anD eveRy·one)

JOANN ♡ RicHARD
"lAUGHter ABOUNDs"

ViMALA ♡
"an extRAORDINARy
WOMAN"

OPen HEARt AdventuRe
♡ LARRy RosenthAL
"WHo is RiGHT there
AT The center"

eMily cLaiRe ♡
"FAiRy GODcHilD"
and AMAzon POeT

♡ WHAT A WOMAN
& SuSAN HARROW ♡
WHAT A WOMAN

WHAT A CAT
JupiteR
"My spiRiT GUiDe"

RoBin ♡ JOHN
"A couple of ADORABLes"

CeciliA ♡ LuLu
"Jupiter's sister and MoM"

GODDesses
"They
GUiDe
Us"

My PARents
"WHo GAVe Me
LiFe"
MARJe ♡ ARthuR

SuSAN BeARDsley
"My BiG sister"

♡ DOUG HALL
and His VeRy ♡
MeRRy BanD
of tRained
BRains!

♡ Helen GRieco
A.K.A. "HeAven"
"A TRue FRiend"

♡ DeiDRe SOMMeRs
"stoRyteller in
another lAnguAGe"

♡ RosE FRances
"cReative spiRiT"

"The yes
GRoup"
♡ cinDy ♡ LAuReN ♡ anne

Molly RoBertson ♡
"HeAling HAnDs and WoRDs"

DAViD e. eARLy
"Peep"

GARy RosenthAL
"My "Being" teacher"

♡ HenRy Miller
"My mentor"

SARAH ♡ FReD ♡ KATe
"A TRiBe of angels"

KATHRyn ♡ AjA
"2 twinKLe toes"

MARy ♡ GeORGe
"MusicaL spRites"

ChRistinA MeRwin ♡
"AMAzinG GRAce"

LAuRA B. ♡
"celestiAL pixie"

♡ DeBBie LAiR
"Hey WOMAN!"

♡ AMeuR Ben ARAB
"WHAT A DeARHeART"

stephAnie DonG
"My 9 yeAR olD teAcher"

My "FAiRy GODPARents"
GeoRGe ♡ DiAnA
"FunctionAL FAMILy cAMP"

163

WHAT IS A SARK?

SARK:
Susan
Ariel
Rainbow
Kennedy

Born
1954
Minneapolis
Minnesota

First Job:
WAKE UP FAIRY
(Kindergarten)

First Book:
Mice From Mars
(Age 10)

Attended
Minneapolis
ART
Institute
(1960)

Escaped
From
High School
(1972)

Attended
University of
TAMPA, Florida
(1972-74)
Majored in travel
Adventure, Theatre

Attended
University of Minnesota
(1974-76)
Majored in
Journalism
and Wild living

Graduated!
School of
Communication
Arts
(1978)
Degree in
Radio/TV production

World
Travel
(1978-80)

Rode a
Bicycle 3,000
Miles
(1979)
lots more wild living

Appeared
in
San Francisco
AKA "SARKFrancisco"
1981

Resident Artist
Victorian Hotel
of Arts and Music
(1982-84)
"Ate too many
Hard Boiled eggs"

Weekly Drawing
Published
San Francisco
Chronicle/Examiner
Sunday paper
1983-1987

Created
"SARKs San Francisco"
Weekly Feature
Drawing and text
1987-1988

Created
SARK T-Shirts
1986-88
Created
SARK Greeting Cards
1987-88

Discovered
a place for
SARK at
The Red Rose
Store and
Catalog
(1989-)

Created a
Dozen Posters,
Napshirts,
Spirit Cards,
Affirmation
Books, Greeting Cards,
Stationery
(1989-)

Wrote
A Creative
Companion
How to Free your
creative spirit
1990

Was
Discovered
By Celestial
Arts
1990

Found
the
Magic Cottage
1989
Found Jupiter
1989

Wrote
Inspiration
Sandwich
Stories to inspire
our creative
Freedom
(1991-92)

HAD
250
Jobs
Ages
14-24

Plan to:
expand my
spiritual
practice or
write more
Books!

Follow
my
Heart's
Desire